Ai! Ai! Pianissimo

Ai! Ai! Pianissimo
Astrid Alben

PUBLICATIONS
2011

Published by Arc Publications
Nanholme Mill, Shaw Wood Road
Todmorden OL14 6DA, UK
www.arcpublications.co.uk

Copyright © Astrid Alben 2011
Design by Tony Ward
Printed in Great Britain by the
MPG Book Group, Bodmin and King's Lynn

978 1906570 72 9 pbk
978 1906570 73 6 hbk

ACKNOWLEDGEMENTS
The author is grateful to the editors of the following
magazines in which some of these poems, or versions of
these poems, first appeared: *Drunken Boat, Frogmore,
Horizon Review, The Interpreter's House, Magma,
Poetry Ireland Review, Shadowtrain, Shearsman, Stand,
TLS* and *The Wolf.*

The author wishes to thank all those friends who have
advised and encouraged her, including her editor
John W. Clarke, Philip Rush and James Byrne,
with especial thanks to Hester Aardse and Simon Wragg.
The author would also like to thank the Arts Council England
for a grant which assisted in the completion of this book.

www.astridalben.com

Cover image by Chiharu Shiota
© DACS, 2011

ARTS COUNCIL
ENGLAND
Supported by

Editor for the UK and Ireland: John W. Clarke

Contents

The Saddest Tree at Kew

There are words that twist the fingers raw
like *only once*, and yet again *once more*.

King Kong, when asked, is a film about immigration
and if you have ever examined an MRI scan you will know
that the spine does not resemble the great ape's
but has everything to do with long telephone calls.

Paranoids are the only ones to make sense of anything,
connecting everything, and although that may not be
flowers, it will be something, just like a sigh
is another way of holding one's breath.

There are burnt words in a battled silence
and if you have ever listened to goodbyes
you will know that they shout and gape
a mouth that slides down a mountain like snow.

The saddest tree at Kew cannot speak or hang up
and rain on its leaves longs for the spring.
The female species of the tree has apparently
not been preserved and in context *hmmmmm* is

a string of DNA for putting on hold and all things
broken and struggling to *mansize* and *beingthere*.

Schöngeist

I'm leaning out the window.
I spit *cherrystones* at passersby.
        I am here.

        That is you,
the insomniac blazing a tirade across Alexanderplatz.
This is me – helicopters in *cages a-go-go*.

This is like me being different somehow.

I *am* loved.
I am a beloved.
I *belove*.

        These are days
when I manage not to think
of anything at all.

I spit cherrystones.
   They rattle down.
        I lean out further.

        There's a hedge down there

        grazing weekdays in September.
An ambulance flies past.   Last night in a bar
I sat listening to people talking about fish.

Why should I write a poem about fish?
People talk enough about fish.

A tree lives for a hundred years,
                (maybe more).
A fly if it is lucky lives to spend the day.

It's 9 am.

    Which is a lie.
I don't wake till much later but I'm still
loath for my parents to know.

This is the life.

    Anyway
I spit the furthest and I win.
I can   'cause you are in Berlin.

I belt out DEARLY DEPARTED
        I AM BORED
I predicted myself –

why the hell no one listens is no wonder.

I spit cherrystones.
I *wishful think* standing up.
I sleep *half a fly's life*.

                You sleep
fully-clothed but with some summer
under your pillow

        (maybe so should I).

I'll shave before you wake.
The tree's not counting.
I look up at the gap-toothed sky.

Now I can see you only with my eyes closed.

9

Modern Love Affair

And that I don't want you to ignore me
is an increasing of the behaviour of the numbers
and as far from the truth as the city of Berlin
which explains blood on a Kleenex and how
happiness is slower than unhappiness
and this a sentence of infinite possibilities.

Language is a map and I admire your paperclips.

Poem for Breakfast

It's raining outside.
The stubborn forever kind
like a door just slammed.

After all you can't tell the rain
to slow down or speed up any
more than you can command

someone to inhale the space
between the streaming drops
or the no wind to ebb it along.

Meanwhile you boil two eggs
for three and a half minutes.
Precisely.

Back in the Neighbourhood

I am here. Here it is.
Totem of salvation in the palm of my hand.
It's a click-o-nation.
I'm a remote control-a-holic.
I click. *Clickclick.*

I go on safari with the aid of the remote control
from a chair that once held court
in an airport lounge.
Not that it helps. I'm still here.

On TV I know everyone. Obama. Stacey Slater.
The Shadow Cabinet.
I am famous in this neighbourhood.
Like a catatonic cat I might be near salvation.

I am glued to my persofonic. My swearing
skilled as any Croat.
Experts say *el problema* is the world,
the world it fits like a glove.

Yesterday I went there.
But my remote can't help the frail judge,
his stamps or the carer who sold them online.
It can't help the weeks the days the minutes flick by

and it can't eradicate such things
as animal cruelty or papal immunity.
I am getting to me. I have an item.
Poetry is hell. People should know that.

I will live on in uncontaminated Nocturnes
in my ownsome *tête-à-têtes*
even though my skin will starve
for the nights it hasn't been touched.

I see my father buried in every televised grave,
a slow wind chasing down the gaps.
I can't remember who it was that said: *Jesus died
for his own thing not mine.*

Who was it that said: *You. You.*
You happiness addict you.
Poetry is hell.
I don't go to bed.

The Other Country

Dreamt B spoke to me
telling me he sees
clouds drift in a carton of milk.

Evening light he says
is a flock of birds
skimming the rooftops westerly.

*

The sky disappeared that night
and in its stead a permanent cloudbank
squats on rooftops.

In this cloudbank small luminescent
baubles hover which I guess
B continues used to be streetlights.

The light sprains his shadow
dispersing me B says
running clear out from underneath me.

*

Across the border the river flows through the rain
yellow comes after mustard seed
every leaf is a slipper *thlupping* on summer.

Across the border telephone wires
are caught in the antlers of the open road. It is where
why did you leave means *why did you come back.*

Across the border one foot easily
forgets the other but that's neither here nor there.
It isn't one thing or the other.

Remember
B says
the border is just a line.

*

But what he really wants to tell me
is that across the border
I want to speak to everybody

and most of all yes
most of all I want to speak to you.
Because everywhere

B persists
picking up the carton of milk
and raising it to his lips

everywhere he went that night
I watched babies being born
their fists tightly balled

but in death B says
wiping the corners of his mouth
our hands are open.

The View

Let us pull up our chairs
adjust our binoculars

on the silhouette
of two bodies rippling

through the folds
of shifting curtains

bearing in mind that curtains up
is someone auto-cueing us in.

Love invents itself. For instance
by answering the telephone.

He pours tea and her head jerks back
as if some spilt on her lap.

Perhaps this is how it began
with a gauche slip of the hand.

He gets up from his chair
that scrapes on the floor

fetches a cloth to wipe her clean
perhaps.

One Moon-shaped Cake

Take one take one. Have some.
The half-light half-dark
half convincing half everything.

Yes she says one of the few times
yes she says *yes*. So that's how.
They circumnavigate each other in sidestrokes.

Or much like a dog chasing its tail in the park.
Or how shadows fall in front on any given bike-ride.
Fingers flutter then blend with the surface of getting to know.

After all
it's only one moon-shaped cake.
That's how.

Tongue and Groove

Or when their arms
their legs their hands
their clumps of feet
entangled

and she asks
which of them belong to
her and he murmurs
Be patient.

Why

Because
he sweet-talks her in places
she doesn't want to be where her fingertips
turn bloodless from the rhythmic
pushing motions with her hands away *away*
because
the tea he serves are wills and wonts she never hears him
breathe at night
beside him her dreams are tumbleweed and tell her *I am only one*
over and over
because
she chews time he hangs her love out to dry and oil paint takes
a minimum of thirty years to dry she can never remember
exactly this dream
because
she has read somewhere six new planets orbit a star five
in a liveable zone only
they are light years from earth and already what we love is time
they spent is slipping
because
why is for Wyoming and weather and cross-eyed it is weightless
and welcome
and also for wasp and for where
because
their love is finding a view she is sick of this small miracle
under the clouds
where he gets in her hair cajoles her outdoes her outwits her
because
she may be an orange peeling itself under a desert sun
when he can't get over *how beautiful yellow is!*

Industrial Technologist

No not an artist he corrects
an industrial technologist.

The art of art is a kind of breathing –
he claims he no longer knows how to inhale.

Besides he has better things to do.
He turns on the TV.

In a letter dated September 1 1915
Debussy writes to Jacques Durand

The art of pedalling is a kind of breathing.

What they do is splitting and mending the notes
and she is tired of stitching them together.

She pleads the notes' desire to separate
produces the loveliest music
the sound unheard the greatest longing.

She pleads for them to stop.
You are always too busy he says.

She whispers then yells in his ear
Debussy warns against misuse of the damper pedal
which mostly means covering up a technical deficiency.

It doesn't need to be that he says.
Outside the sun seeps and oozes from the bricks.

She quietly asks from the linen
in the airing cupboard then why doesn't he stop
why doesn't he stop.

Ai! Ai! Pianissimo

Trees are loose pages
Shadows a signal failure
Your legs are a tuning fork

The corner is a question mark
The moon a bouncing ball
Ai! Ai!

Night has long tassels
Hope is a constellation
The trees are turning

The wind in your pocket
Desire is a piece of string
Your fingers are shingle

Ai! Ai! There you go
In your favourite frock
Parakeets *pianissimo*

The Post Box

I am on my way to post a letter.

I spot a pigeon on the pavement.
The pigeon is limping on one leg.
It doesn't know it is missing the other one.
It just keeps swinging the phantom leg

in front of the real one. Keels over.
Pokes its still functioning leg
into the paving-stone.
It looks about ashamed. Shifts its leg
like shifting blame. I feel guilty.

I lose interest in the bird.
My hand is on the letter.
It looks like rain.

The city is never done. A square.
A folding cot collapsed on chicken scraps.
A journalist navigating her Blahniks
cracks open a thermos flask.
The bloke who runs the coffee shop
stands in the doorway tucking in his shirt.
He's watching her.
Builders are putting up scaffolding.
Or taking it down.

It's all in the letter.

Underneath the post box
the pigeon gives up. It begins to rain.
The sun breaks through.

Parakeet Park

Last year there were 1252 official executions
worldwide. Earlier today in Spain thirty-four
year old Angelo Santomera was arrested
for taking his mother's head out for a walk.
Why is memory painful?

I'm waiting.
I go walk in the park.
Is it just to push ahead?
I'm waiting for a letter so I tramp on.

I pass the foreign parakeets screaming
in the birches since their great escape
and let my thoughts roll over. I remember
as a child I believed sunlight was
made from fingers, and in woodwork

I too managed to confabulate a pencil box.
Or as Mr. Moore used to say
joints knocking about half faintly half
something else: every form must always be fought.
Goodbye goodbye

Building excavations. Children on their way home.
The hours slowly resolving resemble fingers
kneading bread. I enter the shop on the corner and
buy a bunch of fresh mint and a bunch of coriander.
I'm told the two don't mix in the same plastic bag.

Which is when I remember the letter.

The Window

I'm standing at the window.

A bunch of women have gathered
in the square. One holds up a child.
A boy. My father was his age.

The colour of their clothes
in evening light. The shadows
about to wash their feet.

The women's hands keep busy
through the air
speculating neighbours down to size.

The tenements behind them used to house
an abattoir.
On its wall is written *Mabel still loves Phil*.

In front a salesman stands soaping
down his car.
The water in his bucket purified.

I wonder how one blesses life.
Every story gets a cross.
Becomes a member of their tribe.

A jogger in motion on the spot.
He's warming up.
Soon he'll daddy long-leg round the corner.

I hear a window being shut.
How details fail to disappear.
Soon the boy will walk.

He was once my father's age.
The wind catches a piano being tuned
while a plastic bag sits waiting on the bench.

Stretto

Where they are
îles flottantes

clutched

on a mattress on the floor
not making sense at all.

He looks at her.
She wants to go.

I've not finished.

He has hidden her shoe.
Because this is

how he wants to be loved
slyly watching her plotting an escape

barefoot

frantically overturning the mattress
the kitchen cabinets his will.

The Empty Bath

When we yank the sea from its bed
like a sheet off a mattress
the pier
is a broken finger.

Whale carcasses
are stacks of post
waiting
to be delivered the next day.

At night the moon
rises without its mirror.
Every wave now sleeps
within the earth.

Yes he nods
pulling the plug from underneath her.
Adds *Coral reefs. Grand Canyon.*
Soap bubbles and rubber ducks.

Skimming Stones

Some things go beyond
what the human definition gives.

She has never been this happy.
Happy as an apple core.
He has never been this apple core.

They have followed the early wind
to the ends of the water.
Reeds bend over the lake to listen to the ripples.

Standing now at the edge of the water
smoothing out a skimming stone between finger and palm
he is struck by how easily she has been deceived

believing her back to be straight when really
really she is leaning up against the wind
on the lookout for a shoe.

*When I throw a stone into the lake I see no movement
in the water. Why can't I see my love reflected
by the water even when I drop a stone into this lake?*

Maybe you are too far away to see she says
in more of a whisper than ochre –
she believes fingers are quick-silvery bambooshoots

wild and mellifluous and brushed with bewilderment
and that this is why they fumble and clasp
clutch and stroke. Open and close.

The stone skims across the surface
is between forms
leaves an afterglow in ever tightening circles

petsch   petsch   petsch   petsch
as if looking into
is equivalent to stepping into.

Paul Celan Act IV Scene III

I raise myself and watch my hand as it draws the one single circle

Circling it
first with one finger
then your wrist
an arm the entire body.

Chronicle waiting
keep a score of it.

What am I. Meat
What am I. Stone

Nothing. Noting
a circle a score
a number to pick
pick pick.

Slice up the words
slice up stone

eat grass weigh
every word in grass

settle the score in stone
crouch in the middle of O
a nepionic space sealed off
from innerspection

the highest note being
the one for waiting in.

Last of the Snow

I am on my way home.

The street is filled with snow.
It levitates above the paving stones.

The city has cars. They bind the street.
A battery of moonlight swoops like owls.

The spasm of the night. Its pecking order.
Snowballs in a line-up on the boot.
A boy is lashing out.

Who would have thought my feet this small.

This boy is cursing. Cursing it all.
Tears stream down his face. His fists are tight.
The night is breaking on the road.

His sister is standing to one side. Her nose red with cold.
The dog-leash empty in her clutching hand.
She is discovering stillness through the eyes.

Who would have thought.

Like Napoleon she savours liquorice.
They always carry some of it in their pocket.
Including when they walk through snow.

Difference being Napoleon travels on horseback.
By morning his spectre will have reached Moscow.
Once more once more.

We dug the tunnel; B hid the soil

When they tore down the bridge B had to travel back
to his country six times because the authorities kept
postponing its demolition. The order would come
and then be lost in the paperwork. B wanted to be
there because the bridge was from when he was afraid,
cold and happy.

B didn't want the bridge destroyed yet an insatiable
hunger like chattering teeth possessed him to witness
its collapse. So he travelled, back and forth,
as the orders came and went until the paperwork
grew to become the bridge and he was
overseeing its destruction.

Night, although there is light.
But night seems to have a rhythm; it is midnight after all.
Quietness, waiting. It lies there, so restrained and
awaiting the new day. B waits.

With growing frequency B sees a Citroën DS overtaking him
with a man at the wheel and a woman beside him.
With growing frequency they are beginning to resemble
each other – she a pair of glasses with black shiny frame,
he a moustache – sharing a mandarin
while they head for the bridge.

As it transpires, B will leave his shoes on the bridge.
He will jump wearing only his socks. We won't
be able to remember the colour of his socks.
What was the colour of his socks?

But for now, night, although there is light. Night
seems to have a rhythm. Quiet, restrained and what
we remember is what B excels at; how to oversee
the bridge, and all his weight in paper and wait.

The Tent

When you press your fingertips
together your hands are a tent
and in this sunlight glow orange.

You can almost not see the bricks
shifting the light like barges
chugging along the canal

or pigeons swooping through the air
into your hands now open
above the plum stains on

the plate remembering the fruit.
Again you press your fingertips
together.

You have a cigarette tucked
behind your ear.
You burst out laughing.

Take-away Heart

She appears in the window.
She appears to be watering the plant.

I need to be in your hair
he whispers into her ear.

His tongue drains the room of light
pitched with the fever of

is there someone else
is there is there

Around him begins to lose its colour.
His jersey slung across the back of a chair

the photograph Blu-tacked to the wall
of he and she locked arm in arm

and on the table those cheerless chicken
wings flailing in their marinade.

Let's get take-away she says.
I need to be in your hair.

In his voice she can hear
a leaf loosening from its stem.

Fianchetto

Black Poplars
black pencil-thin
black also for the water.

His wrist rubs the contours
a sudden band of red
burns his patinated skin.

In this transition from white
to where white loosens hair
to where charcoal glides

like a swimmer doing backstroke
among the algae
or how slinking shadows

surprise you by sprouting in front
or yellow moon-cakes
his mother sent from Nanjing –

with squinted eyes he addresses
the predilection of light and dark.
Chiaroscuro. He calls it *pure magic.*

His voice taps out
the syllables
CHI-A-RO-SCU-RO

She mouths into her glass of water
COCK-A-DOO-DLE-DO
to you too.

His hands are child's play
are pink rubber gloves
they hesitate

between her
and the image wounding
the surface of canvas.

He sinks back in his seat.
I'm not finished he says.
She cannot say no.

Fingers rap the tabletop.
Gone.
She can tell as he covers

her hand across the table.
Cradles it.
Squeezes.

Drawing in Ink

When she reposes the sketch
in the secrecy of her own presence
her arms lock in an impossible angle.

A Message on her Machine

It was becoming intolerable to be apart. Flaubert

And when he tells her blowing on his tea
steam rolling off like mountains like flies
like money to burn
that she is really Madam Bovary
not French perhaps but really her milieu – *well.*

That she gnaws on their passion
as if it were an icicle
and he the last drop.
So middle middle class – *just so –*

That he has poured her arsenic instead of tea
because really
really this bully doesn't want to marry this bitch.
Yeah fuck you fuck you
this bully isn't going to marry that bitch.

Bucking Bronco

She is tired
tired of loving too little too much
too well not well at all
tired of her immobile words
swinging between them like a jade rat.

She's tired.
I'm tired she says.

Tired so tired of being his rodeo ride
bucking his matchstick legs
jolting backward sideways and up
hey ho hey ho
his arms letting go of the reins mid-air
as he bucks her outwits her outdoes her
when she is bolted to the spot with mats
all around to catch him should he fall.

Thursday's News

Every conflict nurses the mildness of reconciliation
like a hazelnut in the midst of snow.

He cannot stand it.
She's reading the news.

But some of it is just so funny she says
and some of it is real.

In Chicago a young doe burst into the arrival hall
of O'Hare International Airport via a loading dock

whose automatic doors were open.
The police took her down with a stun gun.

She has been to Chicago. She was there.
This is what makes it real.

She adjusts her glasses.
Takes a sip of water. Turns the page.

We watch him process her on the conveyor belt
of his thoughts – *deer are colour blind.*

We stop stirring our tea.
Sit still.

Watch him prompt his hands
watch him knock over the sugar bowl.

She raises her eyes to heaven. *The airport was
very crowded* she says *like a forest of naked trees.*

Palmistry

He locks his hands around her wrists
as if she has no place else to put them
and he nothing else to do. What are her hands.

He sees in them the soles of leather boots
and presently remarks somewhat surprised
they are just so small.

She is shifting in her seat.
He clears his throat
like he means to do something uncertain.

Outside we watch commuters muscle through the dusk.
We watch a dog yanking at the bin.
Listen to the day retreating in the traffic's hum.

Watch time cornering the street.
We watch the room shrink.
Shadows are beetles that creep across her arm.

She withdraws her hand.
Plays with her food.
Plays with her ring.

Chews slow for effect.
So she says.
Hmm he bounces back. *Hmm.*

Lepidopterist

A fat-bodied moth is clasped to the wall like a hairpin
holding up the shadows from the light.
I slide back the drapes, bringing the window ajar to the moon
spreading through the night like marmalade on toast.
The moth won't move. The moth won't leave.
Cool wings beating frantic like an old man
looking for his teeth.
I dream of losing two buttons on my coat.
In the morning, in the *Lepidopterists' Society Journal*
left to me by an uncle on my mother's side,
with shiny tarnished plates
over breakfast – coffee, toast –
flicking through these faded pages I discover
it was a Purple-Shot yet couldn't find its Latin name.

The Light Switch

On the west coast of Canada
a human hand has washed ashore.
It's the sixth case in eleven months

and the second in under forty-eight hours.
The sixth hand is a right hand just like
the first four hands. The fifth hand, found

on a Monday, was the first left hand. The third
hand was found near the second. It's as yet unclear
if the fifth hand pairs with any of the right hands.

It remains a mystery who the six human
hands belong to.
Not to the same person – that's for sure.

What to do? Little else to do.
Read the news, masturbate,
watch a documentary on TV.

No, not on the world food crisis,
(that's old hat old boots no job)
the most luxurious hotel in the world.

No, some asylum seeker
after some twenty-three years
returns to Romania where

the people speak a language
in which
practically everything rhymes.

After the commercial break, his
(the Romanian's) hand presses against
the old front door and then (and this amazes me):

his hand infallibly slides round the doorframe
and blindly insinuates
its way clear of the vigilant walls

with the self-assurance of a back pocket
and the brevity of life stuffed deep inside.
Like

someone who has been far away from home
for a long time can still find the light switch.
Instantly. Like someone.

simon says

one of the goals I have
is to come to silence

this is what simon
says

only not the silence
I know of my parents

says

come. says *go.*
simon looks at me

then looks away
says

there are clouds
in what he says

simon says

while a mountain somewhere
headlong water restless

Stuffing for Being

Distance is an adjustment to the scale
is slightly forgetting the space
the puzzled reflection
in her face not quite he almost.
It is stuffing for being
not coming up for air
distance is the smoke blowing from his mouth
please shut up.
It is the sheets between him and her.
Everyday.
Distance is the photographs she stole
what *I said to you and you to me to I to you.*
Distance is the lemon in her tea.
It is every day
the alteration to the scale
when the war is over yet soldiers continue
to dart across the trenches.
It is here and there
the clock between 2 and 3
and lying wide awake.
Distance is disfigurement
in a handshake
and thinking up the situation *your smile at me.*
Distance is deliberate.
I'm not coming.
Debussy.
It's the final week of autumn.

We are in the distance and what do we see?
We see distance is the gift he finds hardest to part with.
How it sits in his hand like the one half of a pair of shoes.
She inclines her head *you are taking up so much room.*
And he *we always get back to ourselves*
like finishing a book we always get back to ourselves.

What had made her laugh out loud

In Shanghai an 82-year-old Chinese woman has been arrested
by the police after attacking her husband with an axe.
The pensioner suspected her two-years-younger husband
                                                    of adultery.

The woman hit him over the head with the axe during his sleep.
She reads finger and nose close to the page
the man has been moved to intensive care.

The word *moved* had made her laugh.
She thought removed it should have been *re*moved.

Memory of Childhood

When people inquire into my childhood
I refer to the young me as the ancient me.
Because it was all so long ago.

Like when I was little I already had a piano
and could play Mozart. Beautiful.
Really really beautiful. But I never had a piano.

And as I'm being down here on my knees
anyway, dear god

I'm down on my knees.
My head rests on the windowsill;
there's a tailback of blowflies lying in state
underneath the radiator raging at the cold.

I swear to you dear god the windowsill is my altar.
It even has a candle that I lit.
I'm on my hard-earned knees. Praying.
I'm praying for a world in which

not every day, or every week,
but essentially not every day, someone gets born
and that it's not every day someone dies.
I'm praying, praying for a time where birth

and death are still events to be reckoned with, where
sunlight is a bridge across the water.
And as I'm being down here on my knees, anyway,
dear god,

a blowfly falling off the windowsill
might be a violent event
because even a fly falling
off the windowsill produces an impact.

It bounces off the ledge via the radiator onto the floor,
its sadistic ups-and-downs as it lands
like a scrawl from a stylus
on one of those charts that records earthquakes

or a lie detector strapped to the arm
of an innocent screaming
I'm telling you, you did it –
yes you!

Mental or Rental

She reads this in a book on mental illness entitled
On Flying Saucer Religions
and the Serial Repetition of a Formal Self

'… I am a member and owner in the construction
where you are deadened.
In the construction of dying I have been booked.'

She likes this.

We can tell she reads him
like she would the article on hydrocephalus:
one paragraph at a time.

And each time she wants to return this book
to the library a voice leaps off the page
I've not finished it says.

Scene III

He is on his way to her house
a ticking bomb strapped to his back
and just in case a sketchbook and some gin.

And when he's gone finally finally

she unpeels her fists
smooth as milk
light floods the room.

(the curtains are indigo blue and let the sky through)

When she fell asleep it was noon.
While the room
the room carries on.

Where They Choose to Meet

I miss you reads his note *let's meet at the zoo*
in front of the hippo at two.

So here we are standing in front of the old hippo stewing
in its livery flesh on an ordinary Monday afternoon.

Cubed greens and orange peel
bob like bathing toys in his paddling-pool.

The steaming jaws break apart so slowly and noiselessly
we hardly notice it at all
deadpan and void of sophistry
whymeethere.

He fiddles with the rim of her hat.
He holds her by the elbow.
Then he holds her hand.

What are the dimensions in which they choose to meet?

She runs her fingers along the bars.
She points out the weight of the hours they spent
and estimates the volume displacement of hippo to water.

The strongest dimension
she ventures
is the point where sound settles into silence.

She also remembers their Christmas dinner
(so sad so sad she insisted on June)
and finally she suggests
there must be a signature that rounds it all off.

His voice runs a stitch through hers
you missed one out
(his hands fold behind him).

Selective space. People always forget their imagination.
A space voluntarily hers.
That space might be a filing cabinet.
It might be anywhere along the washing line.

Where they are otherlings.
Where he and she are about to burst at the seams.
That.

[The fruit having] a groove down one side

He's from an ancient garden
he doesn't have to write things down.
Plums grow in his garden.

A skylight suspends from the upper branches
open to the dust lightly of the trees –
yes lightly of the trees.

The percussive plums are fragments of –
plum plum   plum plum thuds his heart
deaf and deranged like Goya.

He gnashes his teeth and by the time
he reaches old age he'll have whittled them
down to the last letters of the stone.

Oh! L'eau est claire
Pelléas et Mélisande, Maurice Maeterlinck

The seabed shifts and trills. How water musics.
Washed up shells are chanting runes.

They wriggle with their toes.
They somersault under water.

They jaa-whoosh an arm *Jaa-whoosh!*
They belly-up and belly-down.

Their bodies are marigolds. They are dunes.
They drop on the beach and let the water take them.

What if a whale were to wash up here right now?
They stare out at sea. Lose the shore.

Lift their eyes. They squint.
Do you believe aliens exist out there?

Suppose they don't live on other planets
suppose they migrate like whales in pods

through oceans of space?
They find two baubles on an elastic band.

They hunt for perfect shells. For conches. Whelks.
She has blue nail varnish on each toe.

All day boats float over the long horizon
the patch where they sat taken by the incoming tide

and chafed orange hawser looked at
once more dissolves into the yarn of sand.

Particulars She Exhibits

Friends Family The Man also live in her.
All of them heaped in layers like tiramisù –
the lack of discipline of self-control
the eagerness to talk to strangers

for which she will remain the extra stop on a bus.
And she will eat her supper and repeat
its name the whole night through
tiramisù tiramisù tiramisù.

The tickets to the places I went and the bras I wore to get there.

once more
everything comes from it and returns to it

even elastic bands breathe slowly in and out feign
sleep feign like a bat hung on dusk she listens
to his breathing in and out of what she longs for
the letters of her name *unzipping once more* even
elastic bands dissect are slower than paper than he lets
slip the dark once more she lies *on he and she* touching
her waiting beside him once more ropes of the night very
slowly the ropes of night tighten once more beside
her the man *lies the man beside her lies* the silence
lies she was she the silence even elastic bands yearn the
sheets between he and her conceal the man sinks his chin
sinks the silence in the pillow and further beyond
his breathing *forehead his jaw* his body falls once more
about what his dream not ask falls his dream
once more she reads blackberry bushes on the ceiling

once more once more her breath searching
for his buttocks his back his hand
once more she

may she once more?

turn around you
turn around.

To the Highest Bidder

A clearance sale to do
oh Christ
away with everything
including him including her.

Including the space across the table at which they met.
The bike ride that final day of autumn.
The crystal scream hand-blown
with the maker's initials etched in.

Including also the bones he had to pick with her
the unwanted gesture of abandonment
a raised hand open like stone
a take-away heart
furry
probably German
probably belonged to one of them as a child.

Also to go under the hammer:
a telephone in mint condition with all the words still in.

A bitter fish the bitter lemon.
A leaking teapot
the colour yellow.

All rubbish
all he
all of it she.
All of it bubble-wrapped.

We are also there seated among the bidders.
Consider what we might take
what then might be ours.

Thank you, and please remain seated until the
fasten your seatbelt sign has been switched off

In the event of my death
you have a set of keys to the apartment. Go in,
read my books but do not keep them.
I never understood what's mine is yours.
In the event – please
remember I visited the Arctic Circle
and coasted in a helicopter above a glacier coming
over the mountain like a bruised tongue
and that I got some really, really good sex
(although not necessarily from you).
That on public transport invariably I hated
the person seated next to me, however good looking.
In the event of my death do not worry, please remember
we love the dead much better than we love the living.
This is a gift.
Dead, I will not escape from your stories
as if someone forgot to close
the overhead locker; I will not tumble out.
At last, I will have ceased to desire
to grieve, to moan, to hurt, to hope:
I will have relinquished all my anger.

But remember, in the event of my death,
that in language everyone cheats.
In the event –
please remember that in the event
everyone loses everyone else.

Biographical Note

ASTRID ALBEN is an Anglo-Dutch poet who grew up in Kent and the Netherlands. She read English Literature and Philosophy at Edinburgh University. Since 2006 her poems and reviews have been published in magazines such as *The Wolf, Poetry Review, Drunken Boat, TLS, Stand* and *Shearsman*. Alben has translated the poems of several Dutch contemp-orary poets, including the complete œuvre of F. van Dixhoorn. *Ai! Ai! Pianissimo* is her first collection. She lives in Amsterdam and London.

In 2004 Alben co-founded the Pars Foundation. Pars collects the findings – such as architectural sketches, articles, music scores, research data, journal excerpts – of renowned and emerging artists and scientists and binds these in a publications series. *Findings on Ice* (2007) and *Findings on Elasticity* (2011) were published as part of the *Atlas of Creative Thinking*.

To hear the poems of Astrid Alben, visit www.astridalben.com.

Selected titles in Arc Publications'
POETRY FROM THE UK / IRELAND include: